# For all my dear loved ones,
## past and present.

© Rayner Tapia, 2024

All rights reserved. No part of this book may be reproduced or utilised in any form or by any means, electronic or mechanical, including photocopying, recording, or by any information storage and retrieval system, without permission in writing from the author.

First published in 2024
Written by Rayner Tapia
Illustrated by Marian Marinov
Book design by Bryony van der Merwe

DISCLAIMER: The *Harry the Hedgehog* series is a work of fiction intended for children. Any resemblance to real persons, living or deceased, is purely coincidental. The characters, events, and settings in this book are products of the author's imagination and are not meant to represent any real individuals, organisations, or places.

## Harry the Hedgehog and Other Animals

# Harry the Hedgehog

## Meets Charlie the Crane

Written by
Rayner Tapia

Illustrated by Marian Marinov

In a cosy corner of a serene green garden lived *a cheerful little hedgehog* named Harry.

One crisp Autumn morning, Harry was gathering acorns for winter when he heard a soft hiss and a loud cry. *It sounded sad.*

"Oooh, who could that be?"

Harry the Hedgehog wondered. "Let me go and see."

The crane had large, round black eyes, a red silky head, and a long, pointed beak. He was sitting

*all alone near a log.*

"Hello, there,"
Harry said gently.
"I'm Harry the Hedgehog.
"What's your name?"

"I'm Charlie the Crane,"
he sobbed.

"Are you lost?" asked Harry the Hedgehog.

"I am," Charlie the Crane cried.

"Oh dear, what happened?"

Charlie the Crane explained, 'My family and I fly south to Sunny Lake every year. But this year, I got separated from them

*during a storm."*

"Don't worry, Charlie," Harry said.

"We can find them together."

"Really?"

asked Charlie the Crane hopefully.

Harry nodded. 'I know the lands beyond like the back of my paw. Let's head to the tallest hill. From there, you might see *something familiar.*"

Harry the Hedgehog led the way. As they climbed the tallest hill, Harry the Hedgehog kept Charlie's spirits high with cheerful chatter and funny tales.

Harry the Hedgehog led the way.

"Follow me, Charlie."

Finally, they reached the top.

'Look, Charlie!' Harry said, pointing with his tiny paw.

"What do you see?"

Charlie the Crane flapped his wings excitedly. 'I see a river! And just beyond it, the mountains that lead to

*Sunny Lake!*"

Harry the Hedgehog beamed with pride.

## "Then you know where to go!"

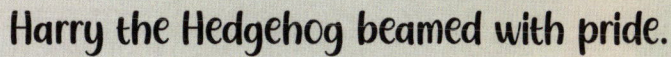

Charlie the Crane bent his long neck in a graceful bow.

"Thank you, Harry.

You've been so kind and helpful.
I couldn't have done it without you."

Harry's eyes twinkled with joy. 'I'm glad I could help.

**Remember, being kind and helping others**

is what friends do.'

With a final flutter of his wings, Charlie the Crane soared into the sky, his heart light and his path clear. 'Goodbye, Harry!

I'll never forget your kindness!"

'Goodbye, Charlie!' Harry called, waving his little paw.

"Safe travels!"

Harry the Hedgehog watched his friend Charlie the Crane glide gracefully through the sky. He felt a warm glow of happiness. He knew he had

made a difference.

From that day on, Harry the Hedgehog was known as the kindest creature. His story spread far and wide, showing how kindness, listening, and helping could brighten

## even the darkest days.

Charlie the Crane safely reached Sunny Lake, where he shared the story of his adventure, reminding everyone that, with kindness, you can always *find your way home.*

The End

## About the Author

Rayner Tapia is one of the NABE Pinnacle Book Achievement winners; The Dream Catcher won the 2012 NABE for Best Juvenile Fiction Books. NABE winner 2016 Best Sci-fiction book and honorary award for Literature, Florida. Rayner Tapia lives in London with her family. She is an IT trainer/teacher for children and adults. She recently (2019) passed English with Distinction, CPD, 2-4 Teaching Literacy in Schools. She is a published author and entrepreneur. Rayner has worked in banking, and has taught IT and English.

Printed in Great Britain
by Amazon